CAMBRIDGE
UNIVERSITY PRESS

CAMBRIDGE
Primary Science

Workbook 6

Fiona Baxter & Liz Dilley

CAMBRIDGE
UNIVERSITY PRESS

University Printing House, Cambridge CB2 8BS, United Kingdom

One Liberty Plaza, 20th Floor, New York, NY 10006, USA

477 Williamstown Road, Port Melbourne, VIC 3207, Australia

314–321, 3rd Floor, Plot 3, Splendor Forum, Jasola District Centre,
New Delhi – 110025, India

103 Penang Road, #05–06/07, Visioncrest Commercial, Singapore 238467

Cambridge University Press is part of the University of Cambridge.

It furthers the University's mission by disseminating knowledge in the pursuit of
education, learning and research at the highest international levels of excellence.

www.cambridge.org
Information on this title: www.cambridge.org/9781108742986

First published 2014
Second edition 2021

20 19 18 17 16 15 14

Printed in Italy by L.E.G.O. S.p.A.

A catalogue record for this publication is available from the British Library

ISBN 978-1-108-74298-6 Paperback with Digital Access (1 Year)

Additional resources for this publication at www.cambridge.org/delange

The exercises in this Workbook have been written to cover the Biology, Chemistry,
Physics, Earth and Space and any appropriate Thinking and Working Scientifically
learning objectives from the Cambridge Primary Science curriculum framework
(0097). Some Thinking and Working Scientifically learning objectives and the
Science in Context learning objectives have not been covered in this Workbook.

Contents

How to use this book

This workbook provides questions for you to practise what you have learned in class. There is a topic to match each topic in your Learner's Book. Each topic contains the following sections:

Focus: these questions help you to master the basics ⟶

Focus
1 Explain why the pencil in the picture appears to be bent. Cross out the incorrect alternatives in the sentences below.

The pencil is bent because of reflection / refraction.

A ray of light passes from the pencil through the water / air to the glass. The ray bends / straightens when it passes through the glass to the air / water and into our eyes.

We see the bent pencil as a trick / optical illusion.

Practice: these questions help you to become more confident in using what you have learned ⟶

Practice
3 Circle the letter of the correct answer to each of the following questions.

a Your heart pumps blood through the body. This process is called ...

A heartbeat

B circulation

C pulsing

b The circulatory system is made up of the ...

A heart only

B heart and blood vessels

C heart, blood vessels and blood

Challenge: these questions will make you think more deeply ⟶

Challenge
4 Class 6 measured the pulse rate and breathing rate of 10 people after they had jogged on the spot for three minutes. Here are their results.

Person	Breathing rate in breaths per minute	Pulse rate in heartbeats per minute
1	30	90
2	50	120
3	35	102
4	32	95
5	26	100
6	40	110
7	45	115
8	33	98
9	38	106
10	42	112

1 ⟩ The human body

⟩ 1.1 The circulatory system

Focus

1   Name the three parts of the circulatory system.

_____

_____

_____

2   Use the words in the box to complete the sentences.
    You will use some words more than once.

> blood vessels   oxygen   blood
>
> waste products   food   lungs

a   The heart pumps _____ through the body.

b   The left side of the heart pumps _____ that

    contains _____.

c   The right side of the heart pumps _____

    without _____ to the _____.

d   Blood is carried in the _____.

e   Blood carries _____ and _____ to

    all parts of the body and takes away _____.

Practice

3   Circle the letter of the correct answer to each of the following questions.

   a   Your heart pumps blood through the body.
       This process is called ...

       A   heartbeat

       B   circulation

       C   pulsing

   b   The circulatory system is made up of the ...

       A   heart only

       B   heart and blood vessels

       C   heart, blood vessels and blood

   c   The left side of the heart pumps blood that contains ...

       A   oxygen

       B   no oxygen

       C   many different gases

   d   The right side of the heart pumps blood to ...

       A   the brain

       B   the lungs

       C   the kidneys

   e   Which blood vessels bring oxygen to all the body cells and carry away waste?

       A   arteries

       B   veins

       C   capillaries

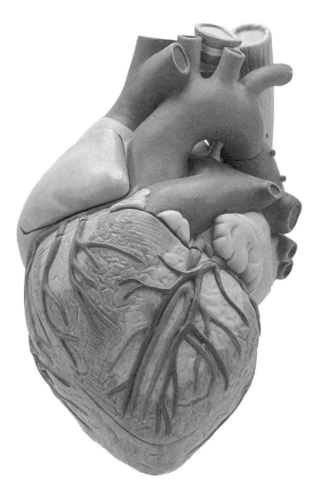

Challenge

4 Marcus measured his pulse rate while he was sitting still and then after doing different types of physical activities. These are his results.

Activities	Heartbeats per minute
Sitting still	72
Running on the spot	120
Playing football	150
Digging in the garden	80
Riding a bicycle	110

a Draw a bar chart of Marcus's results.

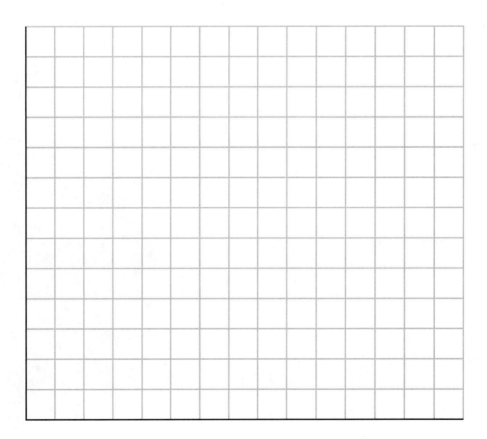

b When was Marcus's pulse rate lowest? Explain why.

_____

_____

_____

c Which activity caused the highest pulse rate?

_____

d Is there a measurement that needs to be checked?
  If so, which one and why?

_____

_____

_____

e Explain how Marcus could make this a fair test.

_____

_____

_____

f Write a conclusion for Marcus's findings.

_____

_____

g Predict how Marcus's pulse rate would change if he pedalled faster on the bicycle. Explain your answer.

_____

_____

_____

> 1.2 The respiratory system

Focus

1 Use the words in the box to complete the sentences. You will use some words more than once.

> blood   ribs   lungs   windpipe
> nose   carbon dioxide   oxygen   mouth

We breathe in air through our _____ or

_____. The air we breathe in contains

_____ gas. The air moves down the

_____ and into our _____.

The _____ in the air then moves from the

_____ into the _____. We breathe out

air that contains _____ gas. The _____

protect our respiratory system.

Practice

2   The drawing on the left shows the lungs when you breathe
    out. Make a drawing to show what happens to the lungs and
    diaphragm muscle when you breathe in. Add labels to your
    drawing to explain what it shows.

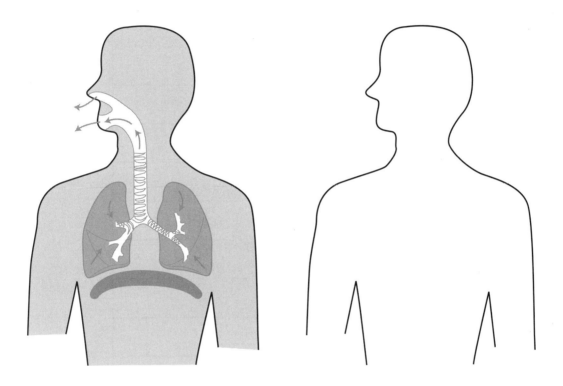

3   Complete the flow diagram using these words to show the
    path of oxygen when we breathe in.

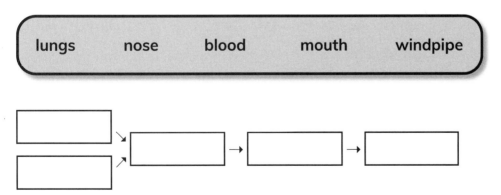

lungs   nose   blood   mouth   windpipe

Challenge

4 Class 6 measured the pulse rate and breathing rate of
   10 people after they had jogged on the spot for three minutes.
   Here are their results.

Person	Breathing rate in breaths per minute	Pulse rate in heartbeats per minute
1	30	90
2	50	120
3	35	102
4	32	95
5	26	100
6	40	110
7	45	115
8	33	98
9	38	106
10	42	112

a Draw a scatter graph of the results. Remember to label the axes on your graph.

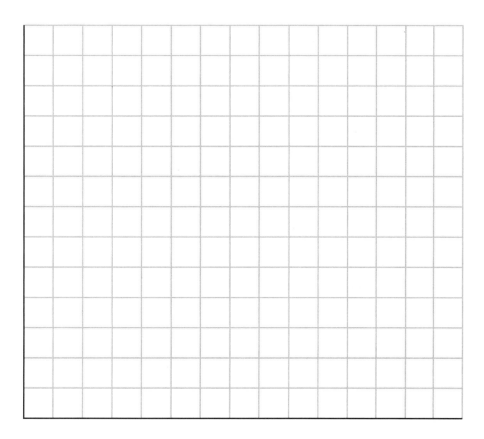

b Describe the pattern you observe in the results.

_____

_____

_____

c i Identify any results that do not fit the pattern.

_____

ii Suggest a reason for this.

_____

d By drawing a line of best fit onto the scatter graph, predict the pulse rate of a person whose breathing rate is 48 heartbeats per minute.

_____

e Suggest a conclusion that Class 6 can make from these results.

_____

_____

> 1.3 The reproductive system

Focus

1 Match each of the words in List 1 with their meanings in List 2. Draw a line to link each word to its meaning.

List 1	List 2
reproduction	the baby develops here
puberty	male sex cells are made here
ovum	female sex cells are made here
fertilisation	male sex cell
uterus	female sex cell
testis	making more individuals of the same kind of living thing
sperm	joining of a male sex cell and female sex cell
ovary	the age at which a person becomes able to reproduce

Practice

2   Draw a (circle) around the letter of the correct answer to each
    of these questions.

   a   Which change in puberty happens to both boys and girls?

       A   shoulders and chest get broader

       B   hips get wider

       C   the body grows more hair

   b   Which change in puberty happens to boys only?

       A   increase in height

       B   voice gets much deeper

       C   skin becomes more oily

   c   Which one of the following is not part of the female
       reproductive system?

       A   ovary

       B   testes

       C   uterus

   d   Which one of the following is not part of the male
       reproductive system?

       A   oviduct

       B   sperm duct

       C   penis

   e   Which of the following happens during menstruation?

       A   male and female sex cells join

       B   new eggs are formed

       C   the lining of the uterus pulls away

Challenge

3   A scientist carried out a study with 100 girls to find out the
    age at which they started puberty.

    This a graph of her findings.

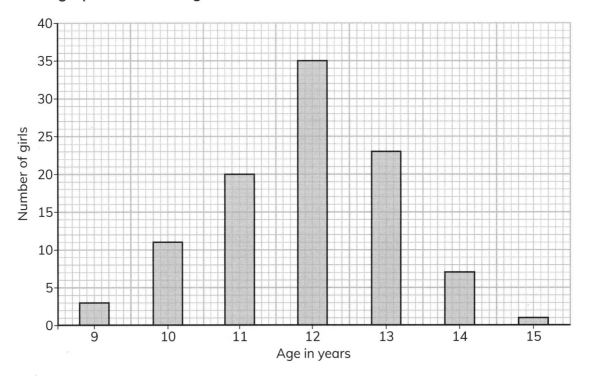

a   Describe three signs in girls that puberty has started.

    _____

    _____

    _____

b   i   At what age did most of the 100 girls start puberty?

        _____

    ii How many girls started puberty at this age?

        _____

c How many girls started puberty at the age of:

   i 10?

_____

   ii 14?

_____

d The scientist also measured the mass of the girls at the start of puberty. This is a summary of her results.

Age in years	Average mass in kg
9	45
10	45
11	46
12	46
13	47
14	46
15	45

   i What pattern can you see in the results?

_____

_____

   ii Suggest a factor that affects the age at which puberty starts.

_____

iii In the past, most girls started puberty at about the age of 14. Suggest a reason why puberty starts at a younger age these days.

_____

_____

> 1.4 Diseases

Focus

1 Mark each one of these statements about diseases as true (✓) or false (✗).

a All infectious diseases are caused by viruses. ☐

b A parasite lives on or in the body of another living thing. ☐

c Living things that spread diseases always get the disease themselves. ☐

d Diseases can be spread when we cough or sneeze. ☐

e Washing hands with soap and water will stop germs spreading. ☐

f Adding salt to water will make it safe to drink. ☐

Practice

2   On the outline of the human body, draw in the parts and write labels to describe the different ways the body defends itself against infectious diseases.

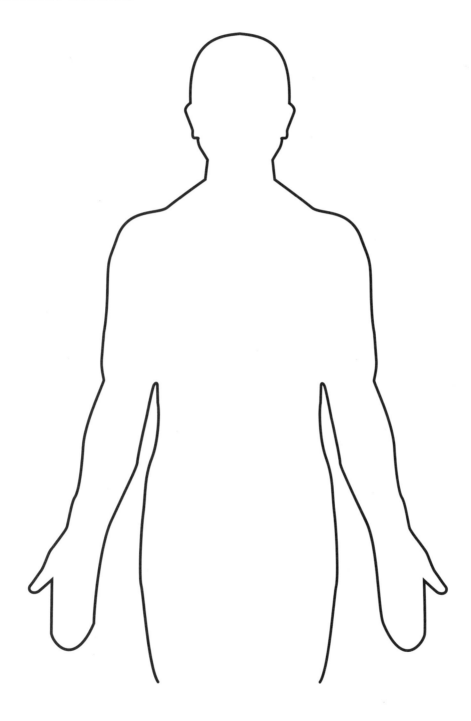

Challenge

3   Malaria is a serious disease that kills millions of people around the world each year. The table shows the number of malaria cases reported at a clinic in Indonesia in one year.

Indonesia has a warm tropical climate with a dry season from April to October, and a wet monsoon season from November to March.

Months of the year	Number of malaria cases reported
January to March	780
April to June	120
July to September	79
October to December	326

a   How is malaria caused?

_____

b   Mosquitoes are vectors for malaria. What does this mean?

_____

_____

c i Draw a bar chart to show the data in the table.
      Remember to label the axes on your graph.

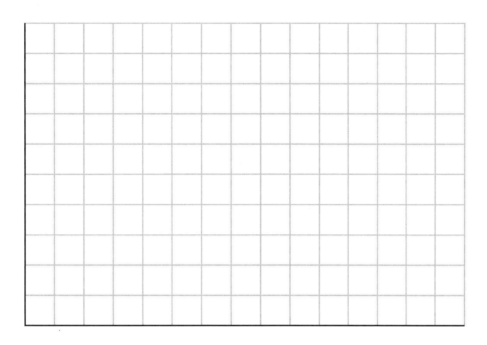

   ii In which months of the year were the most malaria
       cases reported?

       _____

   iii In which months of the year were the fewest malaria
        cases reported?

       _____

   iv Suggest a reason for this pattern in the data.

       _____

       _____

d Describe three things that people can do to help prevent
   getting diseases such as malaria.

   _____

   _____

   _____

2 ▶ Materials: properties and changes

> 2.1 Properties of substances

Focus

1 Different liquids boil at different temperatures.
Explain why this is so.

_____

_____

2 The graph shows the temperatures at which some liquids boil.

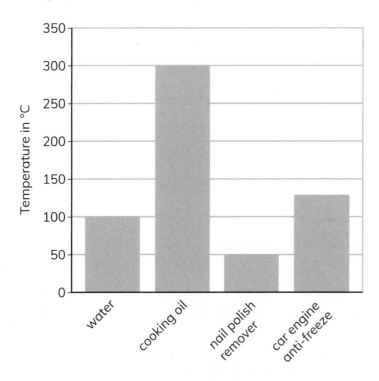

a Which liquid boils at the highest temperature?

_____

b Which liquid boils at the lowest temperature?

_____

c At what temperature does car engine anti-freeze boil?

_____

d Name another process in which the same change of state
   takes place.

_____

3 Mark off the following temperatures on the thermometer.

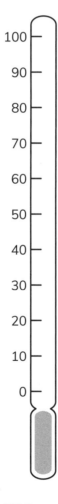

Boiling point of acetone: 50.5 °C
Melting point of candle wax: 60 °C
Boiling point of water: 100 °C

Practice

4   Look at the pictures of beakers of water in a classroom.

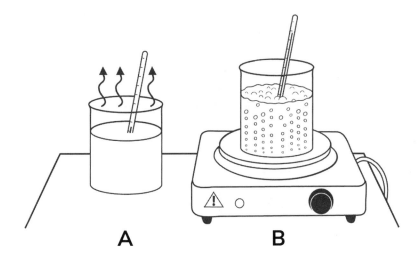

A   B

a   Which drawing shows boiling?

_____

b   What process does the other drawing show?

_____

c   i   Write down one thing that is the same about the
        two processes.

        _____

        _____

    ii Write down two things that are different about the
        two processes.

        _____

        _____

        _____

d Predict what you think the temperature will be in:

i Beaker A _____

ii Beaker B _____

e Explain the reason for your answer to question **4 d ii.**

_____

_____

Challenge

5 These are the boiling points of three liquids:

Liquid	Boiling point in °C
Water	100
Olive oil	300
Vinegar	118

a Order the liquids from the one with the highest boiling point to the one with the lowest boiling point.

_____

_____

_____

b If 100 ml of all three liquids are heated on the same Bunsen burner for the same amount of time, which one will turn into a gas first? **Do not heat any liquids yourself.**

_____

c   Draw a bar graph to compare the boiling points of water, vinegar and olive oil.

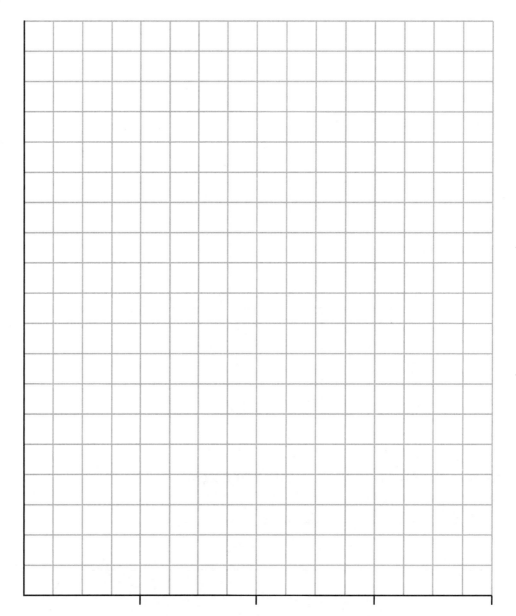

d   Find out the boiling point of iodine and add it to your graph.

e   Why is working with boiling cooking oils more dangerous than working with boiling water?

_____

_____

> 2.2 Thermal and electrical conductors

Focus

1   Look at the picture of a lamp.

glass bulb

metal filament

support wires

wires

screw in

a   i   Which parts of the lamp are electrical conductors?

_____

_____

ii   Which part of the lamp is not an electrical conductor?

_____

b   Why are electrical plugs made of plastic?

_____

c i Why could your hand get burnt if you stirred hot soup with a metal spoon?

_____

_____

ii Why is a wooden spoon good for stirring soup that is cooking in a pot?

_____

Practice

2 The table shows how well some common metals conduct heat. A high value means that the metal conducts heat very well.

Metal	Measure of how well the metal conducts heat
silver	420
brass	109
copper	400
iron	80
stainless steel	15
aluminium	250

a i List the metals in order from the best conductor of heat to the worst conductor of heat.

_____

_____

ii Draw a graph of the data.

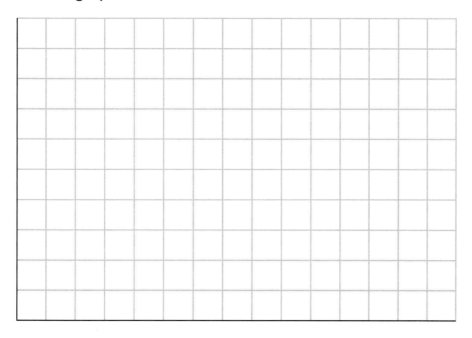

b Why do some cooking pots have a copper bottom?

_____

_____

c Why do you think cooking pots are not made from silver?

_____

_____

d Why are car radiators which cool the engine made from copper and brass?

_____

_____

Challenge

3   a   Will a block of ice melt quicker in a plastic dish or in a metal dish of the same size? Say why.

_____

_____

_____

  b   If you touched a metal dish that contained an ice cube and a plastic dish that contained an ice cube, which dish would feel warmer? Say why.

_____

_____

_____

_____

4   Class 6 asked the question: *Is graphite an electrical conductor or not?* They carried out an investigation to find out. Each group tested different lengths of graphite in a circuit and measured the brightness of a lamp in a circuit on a scale from 0 to 5, with zero showing that the lamp did not light up and 5 being the brightest. Averages of their results are shown in the table.

Length of graphite in cm	Average brightness
11	1
9	2
3	5
7	3
5	4
13	0

a   Identify the variables in the investigation:

dependent variable

_____

independent variable

_____

control variables

_____

_____

b   Draw a graph of the data

c   Why did they work an average brightness for each length
of graphite tested?

_____

_____

d   Describe the pattern seen in the results.

_____

_____

e   Predict the brightness of the lamp if Class 6 tested a 1 cm
length of graphite. Add your predicted brightness to the graph.

f   What is the answer to Class 6's question?

_____

_____

> 2.3 Reversible changes

Focus

1   Say whether each of these changes is reversible or irreversible:

a   melting butter in a hot pan

_____

b   baking a cake

_____

c   dissolving salt in water

_____

d   burning wood on a fire

_____

e   rusting on a tin can

_____

2   The picture shows a test to find out about factors that affect dissolving.

a   Which factor that affects dissolving is being tested?

_____

b   Which factors are the same in both beakers?

_____

_____

c   Which factors are different in the beakers?

_____

_____

d   Will this be a fair test? Explain your answer.

_____

_____

_____

Practice

3 Mrs Pather poured a cup of tea from the teapot and added two teaspoons of sugar and stirred the tea a few times. The tea was warm, not hot, so she drank it quickly. As she drank the last few drops, she noticed there was still sugar in the bottom of the cup.

a Why was there still sugar at the bottom of the cup?

_____

_____

b i What two things could Mrs Pather have done to make all the sugar dissolve?

_____

_____

   ii Use your knowledge about particles to explain how these two things help sugar dissolve faster.

_____

_____

_____

_____

iii Draw a picture to show what happens to the particles
of substances when a solid dissolves in a liquid.
Label the particles.

c i Predict what would happen to the sugar if Mrs Pather
forgot to drink her cup of tea and left it standing for
the whole afternoon.

_____

ii Use the particle model to explain your prediction.

_____

_____

_____

Challenge

4 Zara and Sofia carried out a fair test on the effect of
temperature on the rate of dissolving. These are their results.

Water temperature in °C	Time for sugar to dissolve in seconds
20	90
40	40
60	25
80	15

a   Identify the following variables in their test:

i   the dependent variable:

ii   the independent variable:

iii two control variables:

b   Draw a graph of the results. Remember to label the axes and give the graph a heading.

c   Describe the pattern you can see in their results.

_____

_____

d   What can Zara and Sofia conclude from their investigation?

_____

_____

> 2.4 Chemical reactions

Focus

1 The drawing shows what happens when we mix iron and sulfur.

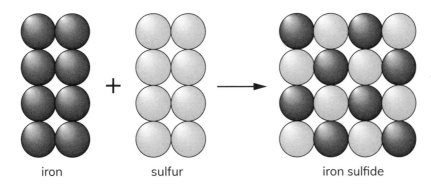

iron + sulfur → iron sulfide

a Say why this is a chemical reaction.

_____

_____

b Name the reactants in the reaction.

_____

_____

c Name the product that forms.

_____

2 Describe three ways in which we can tell if a chemical reaction has taken place.

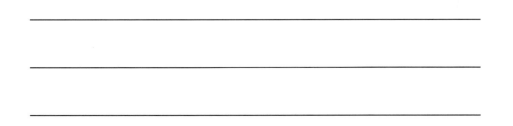

Practice

3 Circle the letter of the correct answer to each of the questions.

a When cooking gas burns in oxygen, carbon dioxide and water are formed. Which is a reactant?

   A water

   B oxygen

   C heat

b When we mix magnesium metal with oxygen, we see a bright white flame and a white powder. Which is a product?

   A the flame

   B the powder

   C oxygen

c When we mix vinegar and baking soda, carbon dioxide gas and water are formed. What evidence do we have that a chemical reaction has taken place?

   A We can taste it to check for water.

   B We can see a colour change.

   C We can see gas bubbles form.

d Eggs rotting is an example of a chemical reaction because ...

   A a gas that smells bad is formed

   B the egg shrinks

   C the egg yolk and egg white separate from each other.

e Which of the following is not evidence that a chemical reaction has occurred?

   A formation of liquid droplets above the solution

   B colour of solution changing from clear to yellow

   C formation of smoke when a candle burns

Challenge

4   When plants make food, they use carbon dioxide gas
    and water to form oxygen and a sugar called glucose.
    The picture shows a plant called pond weed.

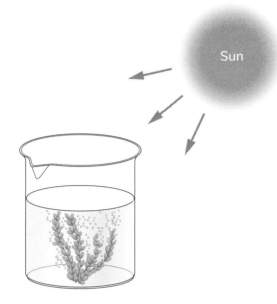

a   i   Identify the reactants in the reaction described.

_____

_____

ii   Identify the products in the reaction described.

_____

_____

b   i   Suggest a way that we can obtain evidence that the
        chemical reaction has taken place.

_____

_____

ii How could we use this evidence to determine the rate of the reaction?

_____

_____

c Where do plants living on land get these reactants from?

_____

_____

d Why is the chemical reaction described important for living things?

_____

_____

e Find out:

i the name of the process by which plants make food

_____

ii any other factors that plants need for this process.

_____

3 ▸ Rocks, the rock cycle and soil

⟩ 3.1 Igneous rocks

Focus

1 Complete these sentences by writing in the correct words.

Choose words from the box:

minerals	crystalline	magma	intrusive
extrusive	basalt	granite	quickly
slowly	crystals	small	crust

Igneous rocks form when _____ or lava cool

down into solid rock. An _____ igneous

rock forms when magma cools down inside the Earth's

_____. The magma cools _____.

This causes the _____ to be large. An example

of one of these types of rock is _____.

When lava cools down on the surface of the Earth,

an _____ igneous rock forms. The lava cools

_____ and the crystals are very _____.

An example of one of these types of rock is _____.

All igneous rocks are formed of crystals of _____.

These give the rock a _____ appearance.

Practice

2   The diagram shows a section of the Earth's crust and the surface of the Earth.

a   Label the following features: Intrusive igneous rock; Extrusive igneous rock

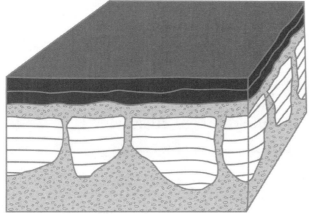

b   Give an example of each type of rock that you have labelled.

_____

_____

c   Describe the difference between the two rocks you named.

_____

_____

d   Explain this difference.

_____

_____

Challenge

3   Arun and Marcus have gone to an island on holiday. There is a big mountain in the middle of the island. They are walking along the beach. The beach is covered with black stones that have been smoothed by the sea.

The boys have been learning about igneous rocks at school.

'I think these stones are granite,' says Arun.

'No, Arun, they are basalt,' says Marcus.

a   Who is correct, Arun or Marcus?

_____

b   Give reasons why he is correct.

_____

_____

c   Describe why you think this rock is on the island.
    (Hint: read about the island above for a clue.)

_____

_____

_____

› 3.2 Sedimentary rocks and fossils

Focus

1   Underline or highlight the correct alternative in these sentences about sedimentary rocks.

   a   Heat and ice break up rocks in a process called **erosion / weathering**.

   b   A river **erodes / weathers** the bottom and sides of its valley.

   c   The river **deposits / transports** sediments on the sea bed.

   d   Layers of sediments build up on the sea bed in a process called **accumulation / sedimentation**.

   e   Over time the **top / bottom** layers of sediments become rock.

   f   Sediments in sandstone are more **fine grained / coarse grained** than in shale.

   g   **Limestone / sandstone** is formed of crushed sea shells.

   h   Fossils are only found in **sandstone / sedimentary** rock.

Practice

2   a   How do you know that the rock in this picture is sedimentary rock?

   _____

   _____

   b   How could you decide whether this is limestone or shale?

   _____

c   How did this rock form?

_____

_____

3   a   Does this picture of a fossil show a mould or a cast?

_____

b   Describe how the fossil formed.

_____

Challenge

Read the web page below.

The West Coast Fossil Park

Today there are few plants and animals along the south west coast of South Africa because of the lack of water.

For forty years there was a phosphate mine here. Miners kept finding strange fossilised bones. The museum could not identify the bones as belonging to any animals that live today. Eventually the mine was closed and the area is now a National Heritage site and open air museum.

Scientists found fossils of more than 200 different animals all dating back to five million years ago when a river flowed through the area to the sea. The climate was hot and wet with big trees, ferns and plants.

Scientists have found fossils of huge bears, three-toed horses, different species of elephants and many short-necked giraffe (Sivathere). All these animals are extinct now. They think that some of these animals tried to cross a flooded river and were all drowned. The fast-flowing river washed them downstream where they finally came

continued…

to rest on some rocks. As their bodies rotted in the sun, hyenas and vultures feasted until only the bones were left behind. When the floodwaters subsided, a waterhole remained and became a popular place for all the animals in the area.

The sea level rose and flooded the valley once again, submerging the rocks and pools in salt water. Another layer of sediments was added. This time the sediments were phosphate-rich sand.

For the next five million years this collection of bones lay undisturbed, making the change from bone to stone.

4   a   How old are the fossils in the West Coast Fossil Park?

_____

   b   How were the bones of the animals 'turned into stone'?

_____

   c   How do scientists know that the fossilised animals are now extinct?

_____

   d   How is it possible for scientists to describe the climate, animal and plant life that existed five million years ago in this area?

_____

_____

   e   What type of sedimentary rock were the fossils found in?

_____

› 3.3 Metamorphic rocks and the rock cycle

Focus

1 Circle the correct answer A, B or C.

a Metamorphic rocks are formed when:

A *magma cools and becomes rock*

B *existing rocks are changed by heat and pressure*

C *sediments build up on the sea bed.*

b Metamorphic rocks are:

A *very soft*

B *in layers*

C *very hard and in layers.*

c In the rock cycle, different processes are shown by:

A *arrows and labels*

B *pictures*

C *lines.*

2 Draw lines between each rock and the metamorphic rock it changes into.

Limestone   Gneiss

Sandstone   Marble

Shale   Slate

Granite   Quartzite

Practice

3   You are given a rock to identify. Use this key to identify the type of rock. Fill in the spaces in the key.

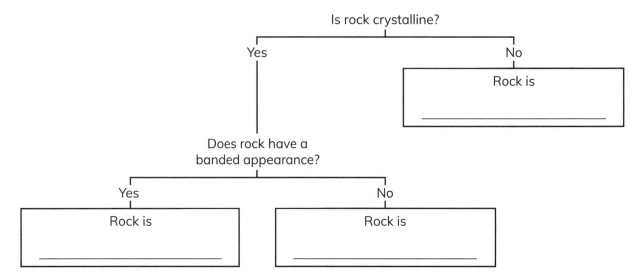

Is rock crystalline?

Yes   No

Rock is
_____

Does rock have a
banded appearance?

Yes   No

Rock is   Rock is
_____   _____

4   Fill in the correct words at A–E on this diagram of the rock cycle.

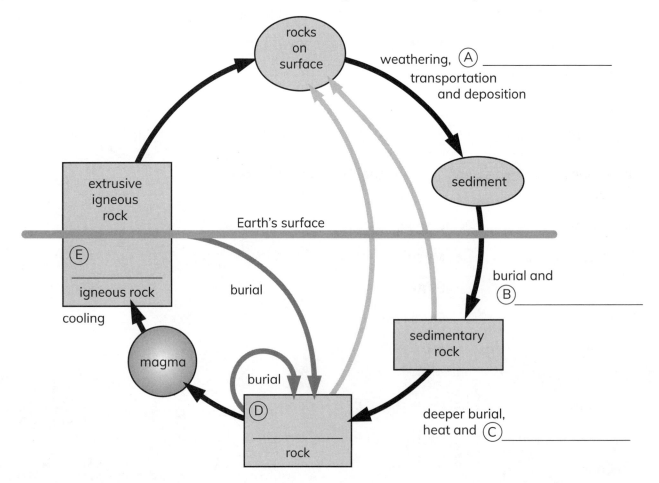

rocks
on
surface

weathering, (A) _____
transportation
and deposition

sediment

extrusive
igneous
rock

Earth's surface

(E)
_____
igneous rock

burial

burial and
(B) _____

cooling

magma

sedimentary
rock

burial

(D)
_____
rock

deeper burial,
heat and (C) _____

Challenge

5 Draw a rock cycle to describe the history of a piece of rock over the last 350 million years. The rock begins and ends as granite.

Include all these words in your drawing:

granite	sedimentary rock	sedimentation	metamorphic rock
heat	pressure	melting	burial
weathering	sandstone	cooling	erosion
transportation	deposition	quartzite	igneous rock

> 3.4 Soil

Focus

1   Complete these sentences. Use the words from the box.

break   soil   rocks

The Earth's crust consists of _____. Rain and ice _____

up the rocks. The small rock particles become _____.

2

List four things you can investigate to describe the soil on the newspaper. We have done the first one as an example.

_____ Colour _____

_____

_____

_____

3   List the three main types of soil.

_____

_____

_____

Practice

4   Sofia and Zara want to plant vegetables on a small plot
of ground.

The soil is hard and dry. The soil is yellowish in colour.
There are no bits of dead leaves or animals in it.

a   Describe the texture and colour of the soil.

_____

_____

b   Does this soil contain organic matter? How do you
know this?

_____

_____

c   Is this a sandy soil, a clay soil or a loam soil?

_____

d   Do you think the soil is suitable for growing vegetables?
Explain why or why not.

_____

_____

e Write down three ways that Sofia and Zara can change the composition of the soil to make it more suitable for growing vegetables.

_____

_____

_____

_____

_____

_____

_____

Challenge

Read the web pages below.

Organic farming

Organic farming uses environmentally-friendly farming methods. These methods improve the soil and keep humans healthy because there are no man-made chemicals in the food they produce.

Organic farmers always rotate their crops. This means that they do not plant the same crop on the same soil over and over again. They use compost instead of artificial fertilisers. Instead of using pesticides, they use biological pest control.

What is biological pest control?

The most natural way to control pests that eat plants is to make sure there are natural predators of the pests. These natural predators can be insects, such as ladybirds, wasps and spiders, or lizards, frogs or birds. Organic farmers plant flowers near the crops and hedges at the sides of the field which attract these natural predators.

For example, aphids are a common pest because they eat leaves and stems and fruit. If the farmer makes sure there are always ladybirds on the farm, the ladybirds will eat the aphids. It is possible to buy ladybirds for this purpose! In the photograph you can see a ladybird eating aphids.

5   a   Describe two ways that organic farmers maintain the
        composition of their soil.

   _____

   _____

    b   What is biological pest control?

   _____

   _____

c   How do organic farmers use biological pest control?

_____

_____

d   Find out the names of two birds and two other animals
    that are natural predators of snails.

_____

_____

4 Food chains and food webs

> 4.1 Food chains, food webs and energy transfers

Focus

1   Look at the drawing of an ocean food web.

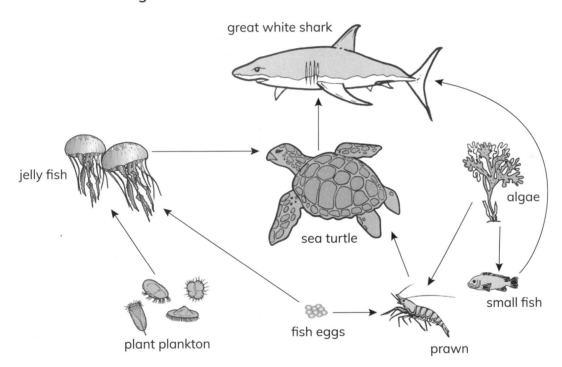

great white shark

jelly fish

algae

sea turtle

plant plankton

fish eggs

prawn

small fish

a   Find and (circle) each of the food chains listed.
Use a different colour for each food chain.

fish eggs → jelly fish → sea turtle

algae → small fish → great white shark

plant plankton → jelly fish → sea turtle → great white shark

b What do the arrows in the food chains show?

_____

_____

Practice

Look at the drawing of an ocean food web in the Focus exercise.

2 a Identify two other food chains and write them here?

_____

_____

b Name the producers in the food web.

_____

c Identify and name each of the following types of consumers in the food web:

i herbivores

_____

ii omnivores

_____

iii carnivores

_____

d What is the source of energy for all food chains and food webs?

_____

e   Predict what would happen to the sea turtles if all the great white sharks were killed.

_____

_____

_____

Challenge

Read the web page below.

> The Namib Desert stretches for over 1000 km along the coast of Namibia in southern Africa. Very little rain falls there.
>
> Many animals live on the sand dunes of the desert. Ants, beetles and termites eat seeds and bits of grass that wind carries from the coast.
>
> Antlions eat ants, spiders eat termites, and scorpions eat beetles and spiders. Sunspiders eat scorpions and beetles. Lizards eat spiders, termites, beetles and sunspiders. The sidewinder adder eats lizards.

3   a   In words, write ten food chains from the information given in the passage above. One of the food chains should have six links.

1 _____

2 _____

3 _____

4 _____

5 _____

6 _____

7 _____

8 _____

9 _____

10 _____

b   Draw arrows on the drawing to make a food web from the different food chains you have written.

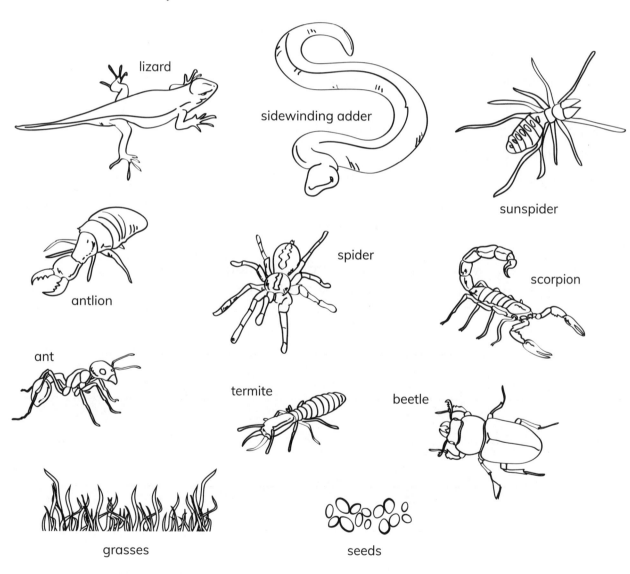

lizard

sidewinding adder

sunspider

antlion

spider

scorpion

ant

termite

beetle

grasses

seeds

c   Explain why a food web is more like what happens in
     nature than a food chain.

_____

_____

_____

> 4.2 Harm to food chains and food webs

Focus

1   Find and ⟨circle⟩ the word in the wordsearch grid that has each
     of the following meanings. Write the word next to its meaning:

a   harmful or poisonous _____

b   to build up or increase _____

c   chemicals used by farmers to get rid of insects and other

     living things that eat their crops _____

d   the air, land and water around us _____

e   a harmful metal in food chains _____

p	w	e	r	t	y	n	u	m	o	a
e	n	v	i	r	o	n	m	e	n	t
s	d	f	g	h	g	f	t	r	n	l
t	d	g	u	t	o	x	i	c	e	t
i	v	b	n	m	e	l	h	u	j	x
c	f	d	t	w	e	i	u	r	m	j
i	q	a	h	c	v	b	d	y	p	r
d	f	m	j	y	d	d	c	j	a	u
e	a	c	c	u	m	u	l	a	t	e

2 Decide if each of the sentences is true or false.
Tick a box (✓) to show your answer.

		True	False
a	Harmful substances can damage living things in food chains.	☐	☐
b	Harmful substances move through food chains instead of energy.	☐	☐
c	Harmful substances in food chains cannot affect humans.	☐	☐
d	Some harmful substances in a food chain break down in the bodies of the living things.	☐	☐

Practice

3 The drawing shows a food chain in a river and the number of units of a harmful chemical X in each living thing.

leaf of pond weed   tadpole   fish   heron
    (4 units)   (20 units)   (240 units)   (500 units)

a Suggest a way that chemical X entered the food chain.

_____

_____

b Which living thing contained the most units of chemical X?

_____

c How many times more units of chemical X are there in the fish than in a pond weed leaf?

_____

d i What do you notice about the quantity of chemical X in a living thing and the position of the living thing in the food chain?

_____

_____

ii Explain why this is so.

_____

_____

_____

Challenge

Read the web page below.

DDT was one of the first and most powerful pesticides developed to kill insects. It was widely used to control the spread of malaria. Mosquitoes spread the malaria parasite when they bite people. DDT was also used a lot in the 1960s to spray crops, mostly in Europe and North America.

Much later, scientists discovered that DDT can move through food chains because animals' bodies cannot get rid of it. DDT is stored mainly in body fat. It also remains in the environment for a long time before it breaks down. Scientists also found that birds of prey, such as eagles and hawks, which are affected by DDT, lay eggs with very thin shells. Humans who eat plants or animals that contain DDT are more likely to develop cancer and other serious diseases.

DDT was banned in the 1980s and is no longer used as a pesticide.

4   a   Why was DDT used a lot in the past?

_____

_____

    b   i   Explain how DDT can enter a food chain.

_____

_____

        ii   Why can DDT move through food chains?

_____

_____

    c   i   Suggest two reasons why arctic animals such as seals
            and polar bears often have high levels of DDT in their
            bodies, even though DDT is no longer used.

_____

_____

        ii   Some people living in arctic regions eat seals.
             Why can this be dangerous for them?

_____

_____

_____

d   In a food chain affected by DDT, explain why a frog that eats three locusts does not die, but an owl that eats three frogs dies. What is the word that describes this?

_____

_____

e   Why do you think the number of birds of prey in Europe and North America decreased a lot in the 1960s?

_____

_____

f   Do some research to find out the full name of DDT.

_____

5 ▶ Forces and electricity

> 5.1 Mass and weight

Focus

1 a   Name the instrument used to measure mass.

_____

   b   Name the units that mass is measured in.

_____

   c   Name the instrument used to measure weight.

_____

   d   Name the units that weight is measured in.

_____

2   Complete these sentences about mass and weight:

Mass is the amount of _____ in an object.

Weight is the amount of _____ on an object caused by

the force of _____ .

Practice

3   Read the following statements about mass and weight.

Mark each statement as true (✓) or false (✗).

a   Mass and weight are the same. ☐

b   We measure mass in kilograms. ☐

c   We measure weight in newtons. ☐

d   Weight is the amount of matter in an object. ☐

4   Class 6 measured the mass and weight of four objects.
Complete their table of results.

Remember to include the correct units for each measurement.

Object	Mass	Weight
Brick	1	
Bag of books		25
Bag of potatoes	10	
Bag of cement		400

5   If you pull on an object hanging from a forcemeter, would this
give you an accurate reading of the object's weight?
Say why or why not.

_____

_____

_____

Challenge

6   a   What is this instrument called?

_____

   b   The instrument is measuring the weight of a bag of oranges.

      What does the bag of oranges weigh?

_____

   c   What is the mass of the bag of oranges?

_____

7   Mr Large has a mass of 90 kg on Earth. He travels to Planet
    Zogg where the gravity is only half as strong as it is on Earth.

    What will Mr Large's weight be on Planet Zogg?

    Explain your answer.

_____

_____

_____

> 5.2 The effects of forces

Focus

1   In each of the following examples, identify the effect of the
    force on the object. Choose from:

    • Makes an object move.

    • Changes the direction of a moving object.

    • Changes the shape of an object.

    • Changes the speed of an object.

a   Zara pedals her bike faster.

_____

b   Arun cracks an egg into a bowl.

_____

c Sofia pushes open a door.

d Marcus hits a tennis ball back to Arun.

Practice

2   Write down alongside each picture how the soccer ball is
    affected by forces applied to it.

a

_____

_____

b

_____

_____

c

_____

_____

d

_____

_____

3   Draw a force diagram in the space to show the two forces
    that affect the soccer ball when it is resting on the ground.

Challenge

4   a   You have to demonstrate five different effects of forces.

        You are given a space on the floor next to a wall, a tennis
        ball and a strip of sandpaper.

        Fill in the actions you would do and the effect of the force
        on the tennis ball in the table below.

        The first one is done as an example.

Action with tennis ball	Effect of force
Roll tennis ball across floor	Make tennis ball move

b Draw a force diagram to show the forces involved in one
of the actions you listed on the table.

> 5.3 Floating and sinking

Focus

1 Complete the sentences by filling in the correct words from
the box.

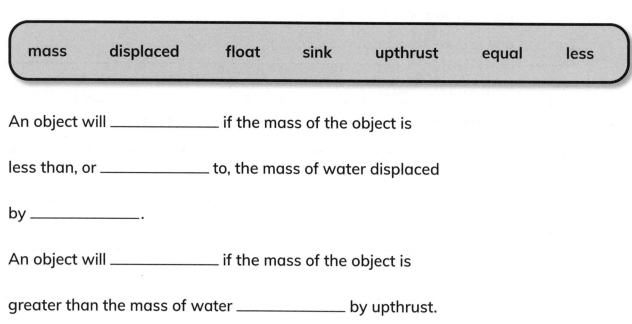

| mass | displaced | float | sink | upthrust | equal | less |

An object will _____ if the mass of the object is

less than, or _____ to, the mass of water displaced

by _____.

An object will _____ if the mass of the object is

greater than the mass of water _____ by upthrust.

2   Complete the diagram with labelled arrows to show why the ping-pong ball floats and the tennis ball sinks towards the bottom of the tank.

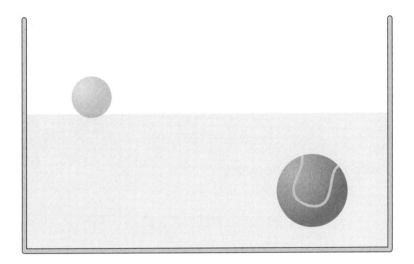

Practice

Read the information below.

Sofia and Zara are doing an investigation to see how mass affects floating and sinking.

They have a glass container of water. They have made a 'raft' out of a square piece of flat polystyrene which floats on the surface. They have a balance.

'Let's try putting coins on the raft and see how many we put on before the raft sinks,' says Zara.

Sofia puts a pile of different coins on the table. 'We have to use the same sized coins – let's sort them out.'

Zara puts a coin on the balance. Each coin has a mass of 5 g.

3 a What are the control, the independent and the dependent variables in their investigation?

_____

_____

_____

_____

b Why did the polystyrene 'raft' float on the water?

_____

_____

c The girls put seven coins on the raft before it sank.
Why did the raft sink?

_____

_____

d Suggest how the girls could have changed the raft and put more coins on it before it sank.

_____

_____

e   Draw a force diagram to show the raft beginning to sink.

Challenge

Submarines

Submarines are able to float or sink. How do they manage to do this?
Look at the cut sections of a submarine in the pictures:

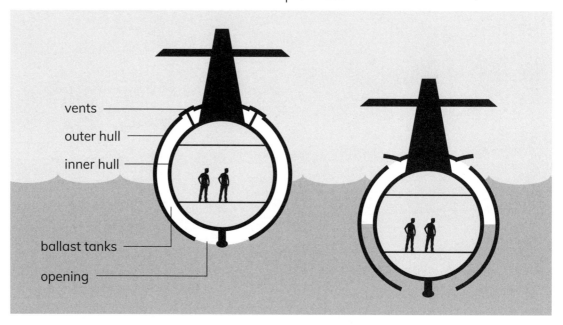

The hull of the submarine has two layers. In between the layers there are big storage spaces. These are called the ballast tanks. When the submarine is floating, the ballast tanks are filled with air. This makes the total mass of the submarine less than the mass of the water it displaces, so the submarine floats.

When the submarine needs to sink, it opens the doors of the ballast tanks and lets in water. The water takes the place of the air.

4 a Explain how filling the ballast tanks with water causes the submarine to sink.

_____

_____

_____

  b Draw a section of the submarine, like the ones above, but when it is completely submerged. Show the forces involved with arrows.

5 Find out the answer to each of the following questions.

  a How can the people inside the submarine breathe when the submarine is submerged?

_____

_____

  b How long can a submarine remain submerged?

_____

  c What is the longest time a submarine has remained submerged?

_____

> 5.4 Different circuits and circuit diagrams

Focus

1 Draw lines linking each component with its symbol.

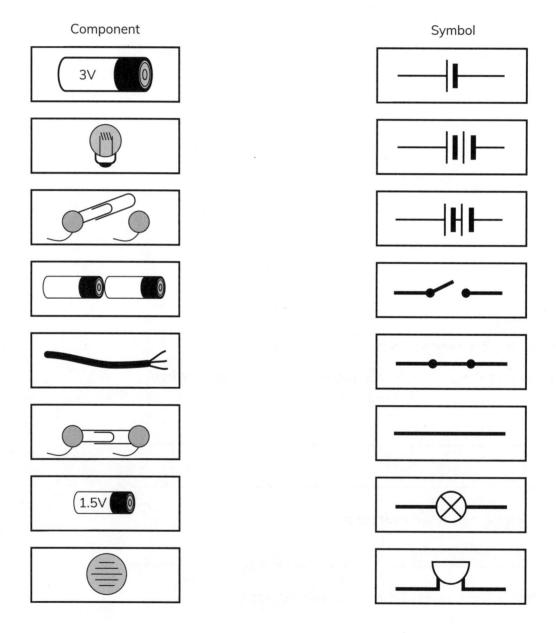

Practice

2

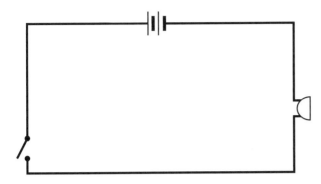

a List the components in this circuit.

_____

_____

b Will the buzzer come on without you touching the circuit?
Explain why or why not.

_____

_____

3 Look at the two circuits, A and B.

A

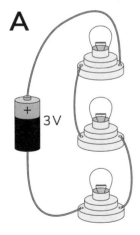

B

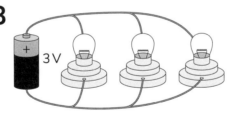

a Which circuit is a series circuit and which circuit is a
parallel circuit?

_____

b   In which circuit, A or B, will the lamps shine more brightly?
    Explain why.

    _____

    _____

    _____

c   Draw circuit diagrams for circuits A and B.

circuit A	circuit B

Challenge

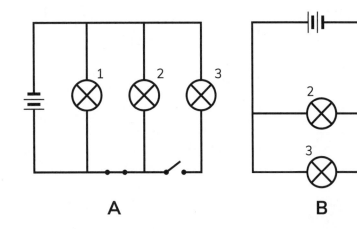

A

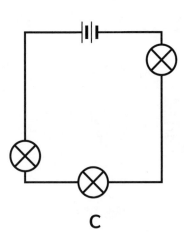

B

C

4   a   Which circuits are parallel circuits and which are
        series circuits?

        _____

b In which circuit will the lamps shine more brightly – circuit B or C? Explain your answer.

_____

_____

c In circuit B, which lamp will shine the brightest – 1, 2 or 3? Explain your answer.

_____

_____

d In circuit A, which lamp or lamps will not light up? Explain your answer.

_____

_____

e In circuit A, what would happen if you opened both the switches?

_____

f Draw a parallel circuit with a 3 V battery, two switches and two buzzers.

6 > Light and the solar system

> 6.1 Reflection

Focus

1   The diagrams A–D show light reflecting off plane mirrors.
    Complete each of the diagrams by adding the missing ray.

    Measure angles with a protractor.

    Label all the rays as the incident ray or the reflected ray.

A

B

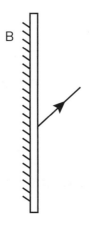

C

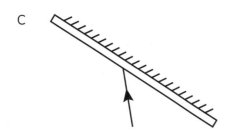

D

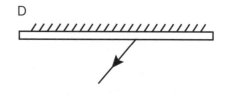

Practice

2   Diagrams A–F show light reflecting off plane mirrors.

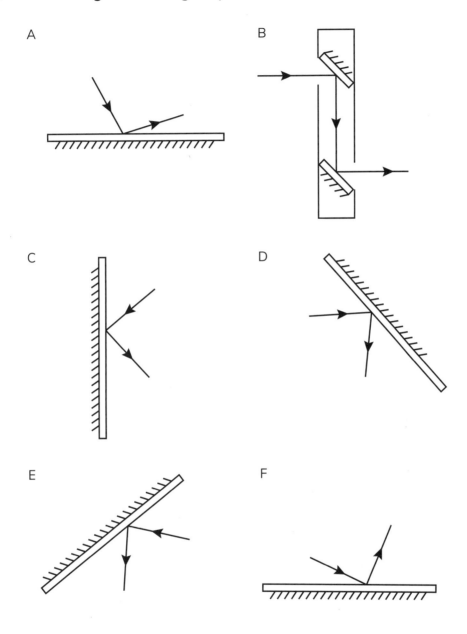

A

B

C

D

E

F

a   Which diagram shows a periscope?

_____

b   Which two diagrams are incorrect?

_____

c   Re-draw the two diagrams that are incorrect in the space below. In both cases, take the incident ray to be correct and redraw the reflected ray.

Measure your angles with a protractor.

Label the incident ray and the reflected ray on each diagram.

Challenge

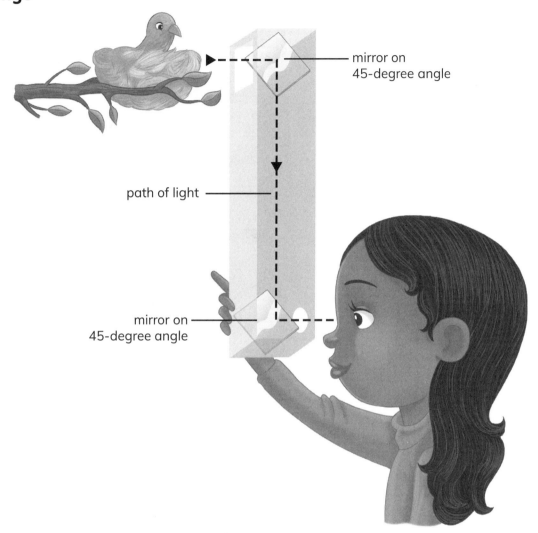

mirror on
45-degree angle

path of light

mirror on
45-degree angle

3 a What is Zara using the periscope for?

_____

b Describe how this periscope works.

_____

_____

_____

_____

4 a The man in the photograph is in a submerged submarine. He is using a periscope.

What do you think he is using the periscope for?

_____

_____

b Suggest other ways in which periscopes are useful.

_____

_____

> 6.2 Refraction

Focus

1 Explain why the pencil in the picture appears to be bent. Cross out the incorrect alternatives in the sentences below.

The pencil is bent because of **reflection / refraction**.

A ray of light passes from the pencil through the **water / air** to the glass. The ray **bends / straightens** when it passes through the glass to the **air / water** and into our eyes.

We see the bent pencil as **a trick / an optical illusion**.

2   Cross out the incorrect alternatives in the sentences about
    lenses below.

    A lens is a transparent piece of glass or plastic with at least
    one **straight / curved** surface.

    A convex lens makes things look **bigger / smaller** because
    light rays bend **inwards / outwards** as they leave the lens.

Practice

3   Draw in the light ray on the diagram above to show how light
    travels from the pencil to Marcus's eye. Draw a dotted line to
    show the optical illusion that Marcus sees.

4 a What type of lenses are used in binoculars?

_____

b Explain why.

_____

_____

Challenge

Read the web page below.

Have you ever read a story or seen a movie where someone is trying to walk across a desert and is desperate for water? They keep seeing water in the distance only to find it is just more sand.

Look at the photograph taken in the Namib desert. It really looks as though the thorn trees are reflected in a lake of water … but it is just sand.

This is a mirage and it is an optical illusion.

5   Use the internet or reference books to find out how a
    mirage happens.

    _____

    _____

    _____

    _____

    _____

    _____

    _____

    _____

    _____

    _____

    _____

    _____

    _____

    _____

    _____

    _____

> 6.3 The solar system

Focus

1 a Label the Sun and the eight planets in the boxes on the diagram.

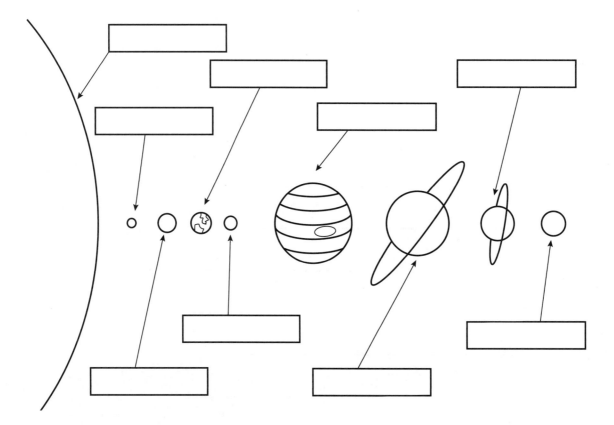

b Name the two movements that all the planets make.

_____

_____

2

| 1 | 2 | 3 | 4 | 5 | 6 | 7 |

a   What movement causes the lit up part of the Moon to have different shapes at different times?

_____

b   How long does it take for the Moon to make this movement?

_____

c   Between which numbers is the Moon waning?

_____

Practice

3

a   Name the planets on the diagram and draw in the missing arrows.

b   How long are an Earth day and an Earth year?

_____

_____

c   Which planets take more than an Earth year to complete their orbit around the Sun? Explain why.

_____

d   Which planet has the shortest year? Explain why.

_____

e   Why does this diagram not show the solar system accurately?

_____

4   On the diagram:

a   Draw and label the Sun.

b   Label the eight phases of the Moon.

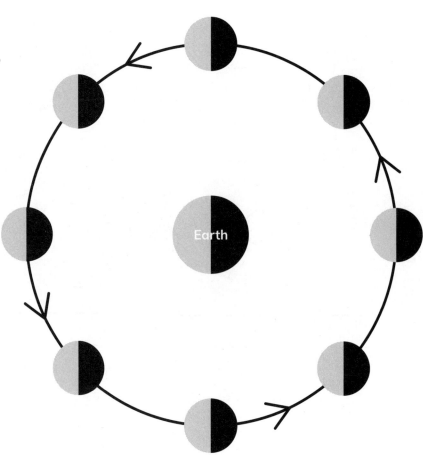

Challenge

Read the web page below.

Compare the planets Earth, Mars and Jupiter

Mars is 240 million km from the Sun compared to Earth, which is 150 million km from the Sun. Mars is often called 'the red planet' – the red colour is due to iron in the rocks. Mars' atmosphere consists mainly of carbon dioxide. In winter temperatures fall to −125 °C. On parts of Earth temperatures drop to −50 °C.

Mars has two moons, called Phobos and Deimos.

Mars takes 25 Earth hours to make a complete turn on its axis and 687 Earth days to complete an orbit around the Sun.

Spacecraft that have landed on the surface of Mars reported a rocky surface with frequent dust storms and no life.

Jupiter is composed almost entirely of gases such as hydrogen and helium – it is sometimes called a 'gas giant'. The temperature is about −153 °C. Jupiter is 800 million km away from the Sun. It takes 12 Earth years to orbit the Sun.

Jupiter takes 10 Earth hours to make a complete turn on its axis.

Jupiter has 79 known moons. Four of these moons are large and easily visible to us on Earth through telescopes. One of Jupiter's moons, called Io, is about the same size as our Moon. Another of Jupiter's moons, Ganymede, is the largest moon in the solar system and is in fact bigger than Mercury.

The Juno spacecraft is orbiting Jupiter until 2021 and sending amazing photographs of swirling gases back to Earth.

5 a Use the information about Earth, Mars and Jupiter to
complete this table:

Planet	Earth	Mars	Jupiter
Distance from Sun			
Time taken to make one turn on axis			
Time taken to make one orbit around the Sun			
Number of moons			
Lowest temperature in winter			
What is planet made of?			

b Identify a pattern in the time taken to make one orbit
round the Sun for the three planets. Explain the pattern.

_____

_____

_____

c Give two reasons why it is possible for plants, animals and
humans to live on Earth.

_____

_____

d   Give two reasons why it is not possible for plants, animals and humans to live on Jupiter.

_____

_____

e   Suppose it was possible for people from Earth to live on Mars. What would be familiar about daily life?

_____

6   The four biggest moons of Jupiter are often called the 'Galilean Moons' after the astronomer Galileo Galilei. Find out more about Galileo and answer these questions.

a   Where and when was Galileo born?

_____

b   How did Galileo manage to find out more about the planets?

_____

c   What else, besides the four biggest moons of Jupiter, did Galileo identify for the first time in the solar system?

_____

_____

d   Why was Galileo put under house arrest?

_____

_____

_____

_____

Acknowledgements

The authors and publishers acknowledge the following sources of copyright material and are grateful for the permissions granted. While every effort has been made, it has not always been possible to identify the sources of all the material used, or to trace all copyright holders. If any omissions are brought to our notice, we will be happy to include the appropriate acknowledgements on reprinting.

Thanks to the following for permission to reproduce images:

Cover image by Omar Aranda (Beehive Illustration)

Inside: Thomas Demarczyk/GI; AntonioGuillem/GI; malerapaso/GI; sarayut Thaneerat/GI; Oliver Strewe/GI; AlasdairJames/GI; clu/GI; mssulaiman/Alamy Stock Photo; Paul Souders/GI; mikroman6/GI; DusanBartolovic/GI; BrianEKushner/GI; alxpin/GI; Douglas Grundy/GI; Manuel Breva Colmeiro/GI; Delpixart/GI; NASA/GI; SCIEPRO/GI

Key: GI= Getty Images